Another Look
At The Rapture

Another Look At The Rapture

by
Roy H. Hicks, D.D.

HARRISON HOUSE
Tulsa, Oklahoma

Unless otherwise indicated,
all Scripture quotations are taken from
the *King James Version* of the Bible.

Another Look At The Rapture
ISBN 0-89274-246-1
Copyright © 1982 by Roy H. Hicks, D.D.
1100 Glendale Boulevard
Los Angeles, California 90026

Published by Harrison House, Inc.
P. O. Box 35035
Tulsa, Oklahoma 74135

Contents

Foreword

Recently Dr. Hicks shared with me his ideas about the Rapture of the Church and his plans to present some new scriptural insights about a "pre-Tribulation Rapture." Some of his ideas were completely new insights to me, which made me wish I had been the one to see them in Paul's teaching. Other ideas he advanced, I had read years ago in a paper written by a renowned Greek scholar, but had not seen in print in recent years.

I believe that Dr. Hicks is rendering a very valuable service to the whole Body of Christ by presenting these insights so clearly. *Another Look At The Rapture* should be read by every believer who is interested in the "blessed hope."

Congratulations, Dr. Hicks, on this addition to your many helpful writings!

Nathaniel M. Van Cleave, D.D.

That Jesus' coming is the happy, imminent hope of the Church has always been my conviction and my teaching. Dr. Hicks' interesting restatement of this truth is essential in this hour when flamboyant commentary is confusing to many.

Another *Look At The Rapture* is a clear road sign, saying, "Look up! He may come today!" Best of all, it gives practical teaching on positive preparedness.

Jack Hayford
Pastor, Church on the Way
First Foursquare Church, Van Nuys, California

Acknowledgments

A special word of appreciation is owed to Dr. Nathaniel M. Van Cleave and Dick Mills for the resource material they supplied in the preparation of this book.

Introduction

If this work, *Another Look At The Rapture,* is nothing more than just another book on the subject, then both author and reader will be disappointed. I believe that you, the reader, will rejoice as you read in these pages some important new revelations never before published concerning the pre-Tribulation Rapture of the born-again saints, both dead and alive.

I have checked with many of my peers, and not one of them has had his attention drawn before to the fact that of the New Testament writers only the Apostle Paul was shown the truth of the Rapture by special revelation from our Lord Jesus Christ. This special revelation was given to him at the same time as was the doctrine of salvation by grace apart from the Law, works, and circumcision.

In my travels many people have expressed to me their disappointment concerning the negative presentation from some well-known Christian television personalities regarding the imminent return of our Lord for His own. The motive behind this book is not to change the minds of those who believe that the Church will be here on earth when the Antichrist is revealed in mid-Tribulation, or of those who believe that the Church will be here when the wrath of God, or Jacob's Trouble, comes upon the world (the post-Tribulation).

The purpose of this book is two-fold: to greatly encourage those of us who believe that before the worst comes, Jesus will take us home; and to stimulate us to witness to, and pray for, our loved ones and neighbors.

The Rapture is not an "escape hatch" from our responsibility, but rather an answer to our hearts' cry, "Lord Jesus, we want to be with You . . . so come quickly!"

I realize that this small book is not an exhaustive study of such an important doctrine. However, I hope that not only will you be inspired to be that diligent saint for whom Christ is coming, but that you will continue to study the Word on this subject.

1
Something Has To Happen Soon

1
Something Has To Happen Soon

There was a period of time in the Bible that was very similar to the last half of the twentieth century, a time when ungodly men pooled their scientific resources and knowledge. They dreamed about carrying out their unlimited imaginations and began to excel in attempting and achieving great things.

In Genesis 11 we read of this time. All the people of the world at that moment in history spoke the same language. They were brilliant. Many historians believe that the Chaldaic nation of that era had even grasped the principles of aerodynamics and had fashioned the first airplane. There are sufficient findings to prove that difficult brain surgery was accomplished during the period.

As their crowning achievement, the Chaldeans proposed to build a tower whose height would reach into God's sacred area. Whatever they intended to do could have been done if God had not stopped them.

> And the Lord said, Behold, the people
> is one, and they have all one language; and
> this they begin to do: and now NOTHING

will be restrained from them, which they
have imagined to do.

Genesis 11:6

God did a wonderful, creative work when He gave man the good mind he possesses. It has been said that the most intelligent person who has ever lived has used less than one-tenth of his brain potential. When fallen man began to use his mind, historically it has always been used against God. So God must continue to do what He did in Genesis 11; that is, stop man from achieving the fulfillment of his base desires.

What about today? Man is more intelligent and creative than at any other time in history. Knowledge is doubling every five years; and at the present rate of increase, in a few more years knowledge will double every five months. Already most manufacturers are afraid to put new products into production because by the time they are ready for the market, they could already be obsolete.

When man can land on the moon; delve far enough into the secrets of the universe to split the atom and invent a hydrogen bomb; explore the secrets of DNA and control creative life in determining sex, height, color of eyes and hair (and do it all outside the womb before the seed is implanted!); there will be nothing that man cannot do unless God stops him.

Recently my wife and I were listening to three scientists who were discussing the imminent possibility of being able to cause a man to grow a new hand if he lost one. They also made the statement that if a person can live another five to eight years, he stands a good chance of living for six to eight hundred years. Bionic limbs are already in use; so is a mechanical heart. One scientist has predicted that soon man will be so healthy and free from disease that accidents will be the chief cause of death.

Yet another scientist has stated, "Control of human aging is something that is going to happen." Scientists plan to step up the process of organ transplant and will even be using more animal parts. You no doubt have read that an artificial pancreas is on the drawing board. There is a new heated surgeon's knife that seals off blood vessels as it cuts into delicate body tissue. In the latter part of 1981 there came a breakthrough making economically feasible the cure-all wonder drug, Interferon, which appears to be effective against cancer.

One scientist has said that by the early part of the twenty-first century man may become biologically immortal. He will probably become more careful about engaging in contact sports, high-speed racing, and other high-risk activities because of the danger of being killed accidently. This has prompted one scholar to comment, "One of the first things that will come tumbling down is religion, because man will not have the fear of dying he now has."

You can easily see with me that Genesis 11 is being duplicated, and God will have to step in, as He did then. This time, however, it will not be a temporary intervention, but an everlasting one. Not just because of surging human brilliance will God have to take action, but also because of the judgment He has promised.

God judged Sodom, Gomorrah, and Ninevah. He will always judge sin. Every nation that has turned its back on God has been harshly judged. What about America? Billy Graham once said, "If God failed to judge America, He would have to apologize to Sodom and Gomorrah." God teaches in Ezekiel that when the land sins against Him by trespassing grievously, He will judge it. Even if righteous people like Noah, Daniel, and Job were living in the land, He could not spare it; *they should deliver but their own souls by their righteousness* (Ezek. 14:14).

Dear Christian, America has now joined the rest of the world in its headlong plunge into the stream of despicable filth and sin. The things being done in the kingdom of darkness are unspeakable, and the Word of God forbids us to talk about them.

Homes and marriages are no longer considered sacred. Women take to the streets to strike for equality with men, even if it means going to war and fighting to show their equality. Children, along with adults, are being exploited in pornography. Restricted and X-rated movies are filled with sex, violence, and profanity — even using God's name as a vile expletive. Soon, a Christian will not be able to relax and turn on his favorite TV program because of the moral disintegration displayed.

The Church, however religious, will be delivered from God's sure and impending judgment. This deliverance will come in the form of the Rapture; the Lord will take His people home.

A great twentieth-century prophet, speaking under heavy anointing, prophesied, "When the Church Age is over, judgment will fall; but judgment will not fall on the Church but on the world. The only judgment the Church will face is the Judgment Seat of Christ."

No, dear saint, you do not have to get ready for the wrath of God to be poured out on the earth. You do not need to store up dehydrated food and "head for the hills." Just get ready for the Rapture. It must happen soon. Do not look for it as an "escape hatch" from the world and responsibility, but it is encouraging to know that we will not come under God's harsh judgment on sin and the hapless sinner. Not that events force God to act more quickly than He had originally planned; He, being aware of this day, even as He was aware of Noah's day, is prepared to do a great work in the Church, saving our loved ones as we believe, even as He saved Noah and his family. We are to witness as never before, live godly lives, and be much in prayer before Him.

2
Paul's Special Revelation
of the Rapture

2
Paul's Special Revelation of the Rapture

Paul's letter to the church at Thessalonica was written to bring revelation to the Church concerning the resurrection day and the taking out of the world (the rapturing of) the redeemed saints who will be alive at that time.

There was great sorrow in the Thessalonian church because they had been taught, and rightly so, that Jesus would return at any moment. You will need to recall with me that after His resurrection our Lord Jesus had appeared, disappeared, and reappeared to the disciples many times over a period of some forty days. They never knew when He would suddenly appear, talk to them, and then disappear. The last time this happened was the last time they would see Him. As He was talking to them about receiving the Holy Spirit, He began to disappear from their sight. They no doubt thought it was another of those disappearances, and that He would soon reappear bodily as He had done before. So they just stood there.

Then two men (believed to be angels), dressed in white apparel, stood by them and told them that the same Jesus whom they had seen taken up from them into heaven would, in like manner, come back. (Acts 1:11.) Believing the words of the angels, they went from there full expecting Jesus to return at any moment.

A few days became a month, then months became years, and still He had not returned. You can imagine their deep sorrow and great frustration when their loved ones became sick and died. Here they were, fully believing what Jesus had taught them when He said, *As the lightning cometh out of the east, and shineth even unto the west; so shall also the coming of the Son of man be* (Matt. 24:27), but then seeing their loved ones die before His expected return!

What about those loved ones who had expected to be alive when He returned? What would happen to them? Now they were dead, and their bodies would go back to the dust. Had they misunderstood? Was there something lacking in the faith of those who had died? You can imagine the sorrow of those who remained. What a time of fear and frustration! There was no New Testament, and those early Christians knew nothing about the Rapture of the Bride, which would be made up predominantly of Gentiles. They had no teaching concerning the resurrection of the dead.

Jesus, therefore, seeing this trouble and sorrow in the Church, taught the Apostle Paul personally. He caught him up into the heavens and showed him many wonderful things, some of them unlawful for him to utter:

> For I neither received it of men, neither was I taught it, but by the revelation of Jesus Christ.
>
> *Galatians 1:12*

> It is not expedient for me doubtless to glory. I will come to visions and revelations of the Lord.
>
> *2 Corinthians 12:1*

The Apostle Paul alone was taught personally by our Lord Jesus the doctrine of the Rapture and the Resurrection of the Church saved by grace.

He wrote to the church in Thessalonica: *For this we (I) say unto you by the word of the Lord* (1 Thess. 4:15). The *Amplified Bible* says, "by the Lord's [own] word." The other disciples did not receive this teaching from the Lord which Paul was about to share with the believers; it was a special revelation to Paul alone. What was this great revelation?

> . . . that we which are alive and remain unto the coming of the Lord shall not prevent (precede) them which are asleep (dead).

> For the Lord himself shall descend from heaven with a shout, with the voice of

the archangel, and with the trump of God:
and the dead in Christ shall rise first;

Then we which are alive and remain
shall be caught up together with them in the
clouds to meet the Lord in the air: and so
shall we ever be with the Lord.

Wherefore comfort one another with
these words.

1 Thessalonians 4:15-18

But why was this great revelation not given to
the other disciples from the beginning? Remember,
Jesus was greatly restricted in what He could say to
the Jews about His Bride, the Church, because of
their prejudice, since the Church would be
predominantly comprised of Gentiles. Had He talked
to them about His plan for the salvation of the
Gentiles (apart from the Jewish ceremonies and the
Ten Commandments), they would have stoned Him.
Jewish hatred for the Gentiles was that severe.

However, Peter did clearly foresee the Second
Coming of Jesus when He returns to judge the earth:

But the day of the Lord will come as a
thief in the night; in the which the heavens
shall pass away with a great noise, and the
elements shall melt with fervent heat, the
earth also and the works that are therein
shall be burned up.

Seeing then that all these things shall be dissolved, what manner of persons ought ye to be in all holy conversation and godliness,

Looking for and hasting unto the coming of the day of God, wherein the heavens being on fire shall be dissolved, and the elements shall melt with fervent heat?

Nevertheless we, according to his promise, look for new heavens and a new earth, wherein dwelleth righteousness.

Wherefore, beloved, seeing that ye look for such things, be diligent that ye may be found of him in peace, without spot, and blameless.

And account that the longsuffering of our Lord is salvation; even as our beloved brother Paul also according to the wisdom given unto him hath written unto you;

As also in all his epistles, speaking in them of these things; in which are some things hard to be understood, which they that are unlearned and unstable wrest, as they do also the other scriptures, unto their own destruction.

2 Peter 3:10-16

Notice that in the same context in which Peter refers to the Second Coming of Jesus, he also refers to the things Paul writes about (no doubt Paul's teaching about the Rapture) as being hard to understand. Evidently, Peter himself was having difficulty understanding the Rapture.

In another passage Jude refers to Jesus' return to earth:

> *And Enoch also, the seventh from Adam, prophesied of these, saying, Behold, the Lord cometh with ten thousands of his saints,*
>
> *To execute judgment upon all, and to convince all that are ungodly among them of all their ungodly deeds which they have ungodly committed, and of all their hard speeches which ungodly sinners have spoken against him.*
>
> Jude 14,15

Of course, this is not a reference to the Rapture, but rather to Jesus' return in judgment upon sinners.

James 5:7-9 also talks about the coming of Jesus as a judge, warning that, *Behold, the judge standeth before the door.*

First John 3:2,3 also refers to the coming of the Lord, but could be a reference to the Rapture or to the Second Coming, or to both.

But to none of these other disciples was the Rapture revealed in such clarity as it was to the Apostle Paul. Jesus taught this apostle many great truths concerning salvation by grace; the warfare of faith; Christ as Head of the Church; the Body being the Church; and the great hope of the Church that Christ would, in a moment's time, resurrect the dead and take the living saints out of this world at some future time:

> *Behold, I shew you a mystery; We shall not all sleep* (die), *but we shall all be changed.*

> *In a moment* (an atomic second), *in the twinkling of an eye, at the last trump: for the trumpet shall sound, and the dead shall be raised incorruptible, and we shall be changed.*
>
> 1 Corinthians 15:51

Here, for the second time, Paul positively affirms the fact that there will be a resurrection and that, at the same time, living saints will receive new bodies and go to be with the Lord.

This "atomic-second Rapture" will catch the world by great surprise — but only for a little while. Just as today when world-shattering events occur, such as massive earthquakes, they are soon pushed off the front page by some other newsworthy item or event. After the initial shock of the Rapture has passed, people will continue to eat and work and play. It will not be long before it will be rarely mentioned.

But what about our unsaved loved ones and our friends who have rejected the Gospel? What hope will they have after we are gone? There is still time — while it is today.

3
Rapture and Resurrection

3
Rapture and Resurrection

Having concluded that the Apostle Paul alone received special revelation concerning the Rapture, let us examine closely the Word of the Lord to him:

> But I would not have you to be ignorant, brethren, concerning them which are asleep (dead), that ye sorrow not, even as others which have no hope.
>
> 1 Thessalonians 4:13

The concept of the Rapture, as taught to Paul by our Lord, was given primarily to deal with the sorrow and confusion existing in that day concerning the saints who were dying. No doubt these deaths were a great shock because the believers had been expecting Jesus to return at any moment.

> For if we believe that Jesus died and rose again, even so them also which sleep in Jesus will God bring with him.
>
> 1 Thessalonians 4:14

How beautifully does this verse support Paul's great statement that to be absent from the body is to be present with the Lord. (1 Cor. 5:8.) The dead saints are with God and Jesus. They are no doubt conscious of what is taking place. This is not soul sleep, which would be the same as the unawareness of death. They are alive and will return with Jesus to claim their new spiritual and incorruptible bodies.

> *In a moment, in the twinkling of an eye, at the last trump: for the trumpet shall sound, and the dead shall be raised incorruptible, and we shall be changed.*

> *For this corruptible must put on incorruption, and this mortal must put on immortality.*

> *So when this corruptible shall have put on incorruption, and this mortal shall have put on immortality, then shall be brought to pass the saying that is written, Death is swallowed up in victory.*
>
> 1 Corinthians 15:52-54

What a great hope the Christians have over the followers of all other religions. We believe we will live eternally in a glorified physical body. We will see with our own eyes and hear with our own ears. We will be able to eat, converse, and lead active lives eternally. The Apostle Paul says it so well in Philippians 3:21: *Who shall change our vile body, that it may be fashioned like unto his glorious body. . . .*

> *For this we say unto you by the WORD OF THE LORD, that we which are alive and*

remain unto the coming of the Lord shall not prevent (precede) them which are asleep.

For the Lord himself shall descend from heaven with a shout, with the voice of the archangel, and with the trump of God: and the dead in Christ shall rise first:

Then we which are alive and remain shall be caught up together with them in the clouds, to meet the Lord in the air: and so shall we ever be with the Lord.

1 Thessalonians 4:15-17

This is one of the greatest doctrinal statements ever made by the Apostle Paul. It is the first and only statement ever uttered through a mortal man describing exactly what will take place to climax the Church Age. This announcement to the Church and the world should stand alongside all other major doctrinal statements of grace and faith. This declaration concerning the end of this dispensation, which will climax with the resurrection of the dead in Christ and the Rapture of the living saints, gives the Christian a hope that cannot be matched by any other religion of any age.

These verses — the revelation by our Lord to the Apostle — have carried many a disheartened and discouraged saint through unspeakable pain, suffering, and persecution. This is the blessed hope that — whether dead or alive — he or she would rise to meet Jesus. What an announcement! Not only does it give the Church a hope of eventual and eternal resurrection of the dead in Christ, it also reassures her — the spotless, blood-washed, pure, sinless Bride — that before the wrath of God is poured out on this world in the Great Tribulation, she shall be snatched away to heaven to be forever with her Groom, the Lord Jesus Christ.

This great revelation to the Apostle Paul of the Rapture and Resurrection ends with this note of encouragement: *Wherefore comfort one another with these words* (1 Thess. 4:18). It would be absolutely no comfort for the saints to be told that they should forget their departed loved ones and prepare to meet the Antichrist, the wicked destroyer that is to come.

Anyone who even hints that we face the archenemy of God — one who will control, rob, and kill us — violates the Scriptures, especially 1 Thessalonians 4:18. This verse begins with the word *wherefore*. In other words, **"Wherefore** (because of the aforementioned fact that the dead in Christ shall be raised to new life and that we who remain will be caught up to meet them in the air to be with the Lord forever), you can have great comfort, not only for yourselves, but also for your loved ones in Christ, whether dead or alive, because we shall **all** rise to meet Him."

But the rest of the dead lived not again UNITL *THE THOUSAND YEARS WERE FINISHED.* This is the FIRST resurrection.

Blessed and holy is he that hath part in the FIRST resurrection: on such the second death hath no power, but they shall be priests of God and of Christ, and shall reign with him a thousand years.

Revelation 20:5,6

Scholars attempt to use various passages of Scripture to prove to their satisfaction that the Rapture and Resurrection will take place **after** the Tribulation. They would have great proof if this interpretation agreed with the rest of the Scriptures.

And many of them that sleep in the dust of the earth shall awake, some to everlasting life, and some to shame and everlasting contempt.

Daniel 12:2

Verily, verily, I say unto you, The hour is coming, and now is, when the dead shall hear the voice of the Son of God: and they that hear shall live. . .

Marvel not at this: for the hour is coming, in the which ALL that are in the graves shall hear his voice.

And shall come forth; they that have done good, unto the resurrection of life; and

> *they that have done evil, unto the resurrection of damnation.*
>
> John 5:25,28,29

If you compare Revelation 20:5,6 with the verses above, you will find a contradiction if you still believe in just one gigantic, massive resurrection of all the dead. In Revelation 20 we see that there is a thousand-year period between the resurrection of the righteous and the resurrection of the sinner!

No, my friend, Revelation 20:5,6 cannot be used to prove just one resurrection. It can only make sense if we allow all the Scriptures to speak, and that can only mean that there will be more than one resurrection which will take place at different times.

It would cloud things even more to hold to the concept of one great common resurrection if we try to fit the second death into the picture. Just as there was one harvest but two reapings — the firstfruits (1 Cor. 15:20), and the chief or final fruits that were gathered later — so there must be more than one resurrection. Otherwise, we find ourselves contradicting the rest of the teachings on resurrection given elsewhere in the Scriptures.

The resurrection we look forward to **now** is the time when God will join the living saints together with the ones who have already died. The living ones at the time of this resurrection will be caught, snatched, raptured, out of this world by a force greater than the force of gravity. The Greek word that is translated "caught" in the *King James Version* is *harpazo*. According to Vincent's commentary, it means "by a swift, resistless, divine energy." In his *Expository of New Testament Words,* W. E. Vine says, "snatched for forceful seizure."

No matter what word we use — whether *rapture, caught,* or *snatched* — it will not change the meaning of the passage. When the dead in Christ are called from their graves, we, the living ones, will join them to meet our Lord in the air, *and so shall we ever be with the Lord.*

What comfort! What hope! What excitement! If God saved Noah and his family from destruction, saved Lot from the fiery wrath on Sodom, sent Joseph into Egypt to prepare a place to save Jacob from famine, and by prophecy told the Jews when to flee Jerusalem from the wrath of the invading Roman emperor Titus so that they escaped to a man, then it is absolutely unthinkable that the born-again Church will have to face the wrath of God or the Antichrist, who would do unspeakable things to the Body of Christ, His Bride. No, dear reader, if you are saved and are living for Jesus, you have a great hope. Purify yourself and look ever upward!

4
2 Thessalonians 2

4
2 Thessalonians 2

There is probably more misunderstanding and confusion surrounding chapter 2 of Paul's second letter to the Thessalonian church than any other of the writings that deal with the last days.

In Paul's first letter to the Thessalonians, the portion dealing with the Rapture was to cheer them up concerning the death of their loved ones and to introduce them to the Rapture and Resurrection doctrines which Paul had received from the Lord Jesus. His first letter so excited them that he needed to write another to get them "down from the ceiling." His purpose was to let them know that Christ would not be coming back as quickly as they had thought.

Also, some were reporting that Paul was teaching that the Day of the Lord had already come and that the Antichrist was taking over. Paul's letter was to refute what others were accusing him of saying. He wanted the Thessalonians to know that he was not saying that the Antichrist, the Man of Sin, had already been revealed, nor that the Day of the Lord (i.e., the Day of Judgment) had already come. Paul wanted them to know that he was not (in our present-day use of the words) "mid-Trib" or "post-Trib."

He went on to prove that it would be impossible for that Man of Sin to be revealed in mid-Tribulation or post-Tribulation because the Restrainer, the One keeping him from taking over, would continue to hold him in check until that Person was removed by God. Then, and only then, could the Antichrist be revealed and take over.

> *Now we beseech you, brethren, by the coming of our Lord Jesus Christ, and by our gathering together unto him,*
>
> *That ye be not soon shaken in mind, or be troubled, neither by spirit, nor by word, nor by letter as from us, as that day of Christ is at hand.*
>
> *Let no man deceive you by any means: for that day shall not come, except there come a falling away first, and that man of sin be revealed, the son of perdition;*
>
> *Who opposeth and exalteth himself above all that is called God, or that is worshipped; so that he as God sitteth in the temple of God, shewing himself that he is God.*
>
> *2 Thessalonians 2:1-4*

Notice in verse 1 of this chapter that Paul is very careful to distinguish between the Second

Coming of Christ mentioned in 2 Thessalonians 1:7-10, and the Rapture mentioned here and in chapter 4 of his first letter. Our *gathering together unto him* is the key. In Christ's day of judgment and power He will come back **with** His saints and His holy angels to punish those who do not obey. (In order to come back, they have to first get to heaven.)

In verse 2, Paul begins to write about two separate events. The first event is mentioned in verse 1: our *gathering together unto him.* The second event is the Day of the Lord, which includes the revealing of that Man of Sin. The "day of Christ," as it is called in the *King James Version,* is understood by all Greek translators to be the Day of the Lord, or the Day of Judgment.

Paul never — but never — said, as some have accused, that the Church would experience great suffering and tribulation from the Man of Sin before the Lord would come for her.

In the third verse he addressed the brethren who were deceived into believing that he, Paul, was teaching that the Man of Sin had already been revealed. He said, "That day *shall not* come, and the Son of Perdition will not be *revealed.*" This rules out the mid-Tribulation position. Those who believe in mid-Tribulation say that we will know the Man of Sin, for he will be ruling half-way through the seven-year span foretold by Daniel in his prophecy, and that if he has a mark, we will know whose mark it is.

But Paul is saying that he will **not** be known. Also Paul said in this third verse that this Man of Sin cannot be revealed *except there come a falling away first.*

As a young minister, I could never believe that just prior to the Rapture, the Church would completely backslide. It never made sense to me that Christ would return for a Bride who had fallen out of love with Him. (That interpretation is necessary if it is apostasy to which Paul is referring here.) I admit that I did not understand this verse, nor the meaning of the message of Christ to the seventh church, the church of the Laodiceans, in Revelation. (Rev. 3:14-22.)

But I have since discovered that there are two ways to interpret the Greek word *apostasia* (translated in this third verse as "falling away"). Because of that discovery, I have experienced a renewed interest in the things the Apostle Paul had to say about the Church during the last days before the Rapture.

Now this word *apostasia* is interpreted by some scholars to mean "falling away" or "rebellion." However, the other interpretation of the word by excellent Greek scholars is "departure." Tyndale, for example, translated it this way in his first translation from Greek to English.

Greek scholars agree that to pinpoint the true meaning of the Greek noun, it is necessary to look at the verb from which that noun is derived. The Greek noun *apostasia* comes from the root verb *aphistemi*, meaning "to go away, depart, remove." This root verb is used fifteen times in the Bible, and in only three of those times does it speak of a falling away. It is most often translated "depart," and usually refers to "one person departing from another person or place."

I have had the privilege of consulting several Bibles from the fifteenth century. Some of them present 2 Thessalonians 2:3 as follows:

> *Let no man deceive you by any meanes for (that day shall not come), except there come a departing first, and that that man of sinne be disclosed, (even the sonne of perdition. . . (Geneva Bible).*

> *Let no man deceave you by eny meanes, for the Lorde shall not come excepte there come a departynge fyrst, and that synful man be opened, the sonne of perdicyon. . . (Great Bible).*

> *Let no man deceave you by eny meanes, for the Lorde commeth not, excepte ther come a departinge fyrst, and that that synfull man be opened, the sonne of perdicion. . . (Tyndale).*

Then we come to the translation of an excellent, widely recognized commentator, Kenneth S. Wuest.

In *The New Testament — An Expanded Translation,*
Mr. Wuest translates 2 Thessalonians 2:3 as follows:

> Do not begin to allow anyone to lead
> you astray in any way, because that day
> shall not come except the aforementioned
> departure [of the Church to heaven] comes
> first and the man of the lawlessness is
> disclosed [in his true identity], the man of
> perdition. . . .

The definite article occurring before the word
apostasia makes it apply to a particular departure,
one known to the writer and the recipients of the
letter.

John Dawson, A.B., indicates that *apostasia*
means a departure from any place.

John Lineberry, B.A., translates
2 Thessalonians 2:3 thusly:

> Do not begin to let anyone beguile you
> in any way, because the day will not come
> (day of the Lord) except there come the
> departure (rapture of the Church first) and
> the man of lawlessness be revealed
> (unveiled, uncovered) the son of perdition
> (eternal misery, doom and destruction).

The following is a list of others who use the
word *departure:*

Coverdale (1535)

Crammer (1539)

Beza (1565)

Rev. J. R. Major, M.A. (1831)

John James, L.L.D. (1825)

Robert Baker, *Breechers Bible* (1615)

John Parkhurst (1851) **Lexicon — London**

"Properly, a departure." Third meaning: "A divorce or dismission."

Robert Scott (1811-1887) **Oxford Press**

Second meaning: "Departure; disappearance."

James Donnegan, M.D., Greek/English Lexicon

The Amplified Bible, New Testament footnote

These excellent Greek scholars and commentators give us sufficient evidence to know of a certainty that this Greek word *apostasia* can be rightfully translated in more ways than one; "departure" best fits into this context.

I will be happy to acknowledge that our hope in the pre-Tribulation Rapture does not hinge on how one Greek word is translated, but this translation certainly ties in beautifully with the rest of the chapter.

And now ye know what withholdeth that he might be revealed in his time.

> For the mystery of iniquity doth
> already work: only he who now letteth will
> let, until he be taken out of the way.
>
> > *2 Thessalonians 2:6,7*

Most Bible commentators agree that "he who now letteth" (the One Who now restrains the Antichrist from appearing) is the Holy Spirit. It will not be necessary to take the space here to relate all those who believe this, and why, but there are many.

The Holy Spirit is the life *(zoe)* of the Church. In John 14:16 Jesus promised the Church that when the Holy Spirit came, He would *abide with you for ever.* So, when He is *taken out of the way* (v. 7), we have to go with Him, for without Him we have no life. John 6:63 states: *It is the spirit that quickeneth* (Gr. *zoopoieo*, "to make alive, give life, quicken"). If the Holy Spirit stepped aside to allow the Antichrist to be revealed before the Rapture, then all the spiritual life in the Church would cease. And if the Holy Spirit left without us, the Scriptures would be broken, for Jesus promised that He, the Holy Spirit, would abide with us forever.

Some have held that the Antichrist is holding himself back from being revealed. In his commentary Dr. T. J. McCrossan says that anyone suggesting such a thing is utterly ignorant of Greek grammar. No, it isn't the Antichrist restraining himself.

Others holding the post-Tribulation position say that the "he" of verse 6 refers to the Roman government. If the Roman government had been the one restraining the Antichrist, he would have taken over when Rome fell. This restrainer is a person, not a form of government. In order to be able to hold back the Antichrist, this person must be bigger and stronger than the Antichrist. Therefore, it must be the Holy Spirit.

Neither could the restrainer be the Church. The Greek word for the Church is *ekklesia,* which is of the feminine gender. Greek scholars tell us that there is a hard and fast law in Greek grammar which states that the article and participle must agree in gender, number, and case with the nouns they qualify. *Ho katechon* (the one holding back) is masculine and therefore refers to the Holy Spirit (also masculine) and not to the Church.

Dr. McCrossan's exact translation of Colossians 3:4 states: *When Christ, the life of us (he zoe hemon), may be manifested then shall ye (the saints) be manifested together with Him in glory.*

Until that great day in glory comes, we must rely on the blessed work of the Holy Spirit to sustain us. There could be no life if He were to step aside. Berry's *Interlinear Greek-English New Testament* gives the literal meaning of "taken out" as "out of the midst he be gone." How could He just step aside when His presence fills the earth? No, when He is "taken out," He will be taken out completely, and we will be gathered to the Lord with Him.

At that time, then, Satan will have full power (*dunamis*) in the world. As of now, since the Cross, he has only limited power (*exousia*). Satan will give his unrestrained power to the Antichrist. The Church cannot be here when that happens, because it would violate Matthew 18:18: *Verily I say unto you, Whatsoever ye shall bind on earth shall be bound in heaven: and whatsoever ye shall loose on earth shall be loosed in heaven.* The Church left on earth without the Holy Spirit could no longer have the power to bind and loose because the Antichrist will have full power when he rules and deceives.

It is regrettable that so much confusion has risen from Paul's second letter to the church in Thessalonica. Just as Paul was falsely interpreted in his day, so the problem continues. There are many well-known radio and television personalities proclaiming that the Church will either go half-way or all the way through the Tribulation. The confusion arises when Paul's special revelation of the Rapture of the Church is combined with Matthew 24 (which describes the destruction of the Jewish temple) and Daniel's prophecy of the end times.

Daniel 9:27 describes the seventieth week — seven years of horror. This time period is also described in Revelation; the first three and one-half years will be peaceable, but the second three and one-half years will be a holocaust greater than anything man has ever witnessed.

Paul did not say then, nor does the Bible teach that Paul was saying, that we, the Church, will be there when the Antichrist is manifested. Luke 21:36 says: *Watch ye therefore, and pray always, that ye may be accounted worthy TO ESCAPE all these things that shall come to pass, and to stand before the Son of man.* The Greek word *ekpheugo* which is translated here "to escape" means "to escape clean away from."

No, dear reader, you do not have to head for the hills with a seven-year supply of dehydrated food and guns to protect it. Our Lord has never thrown us to the wolves, and He is not going to do so at the end of the Church Age.

And, no, the Church is **not** perfected by suffering, as we hear some teach. Some say that the Church isn't ready to stand before God so it needs to be purged by the Tribulation. Dearly beloved, don't buy this nonsense. If the blood of Jesus Christ, God's Son, does not qualify you for heaven, then having your head cut off, dying of starvation, or suffering in prison will not qualify you either. Remember this truth: All the thief on the cross needed to make himself worthy to be with Jesus was to say, *Remember me* (Luke 23:42). In other words, "I believe in You and want to go with You." That simple faith qualified him for heaven, and equally so, it qualifies every person who has accepted Christ for 2,000 years.

All the dead saints who have gone on before us, having put their trust in Jesus' blood, will come back with Him to get their bodies and will ascend ahead of us. They did not need the Antichrist to take over in order to get them ready, and neither do we. They did not have to have a special work done in them to ready them for the Rapture, and neither do we. There is no difference in the eyes of God between a dead saint and a living one. Everyone there will be present because of the blood atonement of our Lord Jesus.

> *Much more then, being now justified by his blood, we shall be SAVED FROM WRATH through him.*
>
> Romans 5:9

> *But as many as received him, to them gave he power to become the sons of God, even to them that believe on his name.*
>
> John 1:12

Abraham believed God and God counted him to be righteous. (Rom. 4:3.) That is all he needed, and it is all we need.

Reader, believe in Him. . . trust in Him. . . receive Him as your Lord and Savior, if you desire to go up with the saints of all ages when He comes for His Bride.

One final word about the concept of using the word *departure* instead of *falling away.* Peter's

sermon on the day of the outpouring of the Holy
Spirit refers to Joel 2:28,29. He said, *It shall come to
pass in the last days* (Acts 2:17). What shall come to
pass in the last days? A great falling away? Never;
no, never! What will come to pass, even beginning
then, is **a mighty outpouring of the Holy Spirit** on all
flesh. A person who insists on the use of "falling
away" in 2 Thessalonians 2:3 and who sees the
Church in rebellion has contradicted Peter's sermon,
the Old Testament prophecy from Joel, and just good
common sense.

No, do not prepare for the Antichrist. Prepare
your heart to meet Jesus and witness, as never
before, to a dying world.

5
The Church Will Not Be Surprised

5
The Church Will Not Be Surprised

In 1 Thessalonians 5, the Apostle Paul continues to expound on his revelation from Jesus concerning the Rapture, a unique word of revelation as fresh as that of salvation by grace apart from the law of Moses and circumcision.

> For yourselves know perfectly that the day of the Lord so cometh as a thief in the night.
>
> For when they (the world) shall say, Peace and safety; then sudden destruction cometh upon them, as travail upon a woman with child; and they shall not escape.
>
> 1 Thessalonians 5:2,3

The world will think they have truly attained earthly utopia. All is well at last! They have a new leader and have really arrived. That is when the bottom will drop out and the roof will cave in. They, the Christ-rejecting ones, will not escape. Destruction will come suddenly upon them without the slightest warning.

Notice carefully that judgment will come upon them, the world, as a thief comes in the night —

unannounced! **But verse 4 plainly teaches us that it will not be that way with the Church:**

> *But you are not in [given up to the power of] darkness, brethren, for that day to overtake you by surprise like a thief.*
> *1 Thessalonians 5:4 AMP*

That day will not slip up on us. Why? Because we are children of the light and of the day. We will not be drunken or asleep, neither will we be surprised. You may say, "What are you saying? I have heard all my life that the Rapture will come on us as a thief in the night. I have heard all my life that no man knows the day or the hour — no, not even the angels, or the Son. Only the Father knows."

That teaching is based on Matthew 24:36:

> *But of that day and hour knoweth no man, no, not the angels of heaven, but my Father only.*

This scripture is in the context of end times and **judgment.** If it is not, then you have just found the first doctrinal contradiction in the Bible because we have just seen where the Apostle Paul says in 1 Thessalonians 5:4 that the Church, the Bride of Christ, will not be set upon as the victim of a thief.

But there is no contradiction because these two passages deal with two entirely different events and two entirely different groups of people. The twenty-fourth chapter of Matthew is an account of **judgment on the Jewish nation** for their rejection and crucifixion of Jesus. First Thessalonians 5:2,3 relates to **judgment on the whole world** which remains **after** the Rapture. Matthew 24 is a great contrast to the time of the Rapture, and in no way can be compared to 1 Thessalonians 5.

The signs of the last day will be very obvious to the Christian; they are comparable to the signs in the days of Noah and Lot. The Gentile Church is promised a **heavenly** kingdom, and they will be looking for such to be revealed.

The Jewish nation, on the other hand, is not looking for the return of the Messiah; they are promised an **earthly** kingdom. Daniel's vision of the sixty-nine weeks was Jewish. (Dan. 9.) The seventieth week (seven years) is also allotted to the Jews and is called the "time of Jacob's Trouble." The Christ-rejecting nation of Israel is headed for that time of Jacob's Trouble before they come back to a day of glory, their earthly kingdom.

> *For thus saith the Lord; We have heard a voice of trembling, of fear, and not of peace.*

> *Ask ye now, and see whether a man doth travail with child? wherefore do I see every man with his hands on his loins, as a woman in travail, and all faces are turned into paleness?*

> *Alas! for that day is great, so that none is like it: it is even the time of Jacob's trouble; but he shall be saved out of it* (that is, the 144,000 of Revelation 7).
>
> *Jeremiah 30:5-7*

> *And shall cut him asunder, and appoint him his portion with the hypocrites: there shall be weeping and gnashing of teeth.*
>
> *Matthew 24:51*

(See also Joel 2:11-31 and Zephaniah 1:14.)

This future holocaust will by far surpass anything the Jewish nation has ever witnessed, including the concentration camps of World War II. Only 144,000 of them will be saved. (Rev. 7.)

Post-Tribulation interpreters do not foresee the Church's escaping the wrath poured out in the book of Revelation. I cannot accept this interpretation because, along with many others, I believe that John's visit to heaven in the spirit follows the Rapture of the Church. John saw this vision symbolically, and it is recorded in Revelation 4. He saw the twenty-four elders with gold crowns on their heads. (v. 4.) This means that the Rapture had already taken place and the Judgment Seat of Christ had been completed. The crowns and rewards had **already** been given to the faithful overcomers, the Church.

In Revelation 5, the book is opened and the redeemed sing that they will return to earth to rule and reign, and they will number *ten thousand times ten thousand, and thousands of thousands* (v. 11). Chapters 4 and 5 no doubt occupy the seven years; the last three and one-half years of the seven being the time of Jacob's Trouble and God's wrath being poured out on the earth, which is recorded in the rest of the book of Revelation.

> *For God hath NOT appointed us to wrath, but to obtain salvation by our Lord Jesus Christ.*
>
> 1 Thessalonians 5:9

This verse makes it very clear that the Church is **not** appointed for the time of wrath, but to obtain salvation (deliverance), as is indicated by Jesus' own words in Revelation 3:10 AMP:

> *. . .I also will keep you (safe) from the hour of trial (testing) which is coming on the whole world. . . .*

The Living Bible states this verse: *I will protect you from the time of Great Tribulation and Temptation, which will come upon the world.*

No, good Christian brother and sister, we have greatly erred in mixing together the Second Coming of Christ with the Rapture. **That glorious event will not catch us by surprise. We, the redeemed of the Lord, will share His secret:**

Another Look At The Rapture

> *Surely the Lord God will do nothing but he revealeth HIS SECRET unto his servants the prophets.*
>
> *Amos 3:7*

You might ask, "What do you think we will know, inasmuch as we are not going to be surprised?" That question cannot be fully answered. We are not told what we will know. We only know that we will not be surprised by the Rapture.

The world will be shocked. But we, as we rise, may look at one another and say, "I am glad it happened today. . . but I thought it would happen yesterday!" Maybe, as the day comes nearer, we will all just go around witnessing for our Lord, business as usual, but with a special, distinctive look on our faces. Our conversation might be about whether we think it will be today that He comes, or whether it will be tomorrow.

Perhaps "Rapture parties" of praise and worship will become daily or weekly events among believers! As that day draws nearer and nearer and the time becomes shorter (as we run out of both time and distance), we will be walking with God as Enoch of old, and God will take us, and that not by surprise.

> *. . . and unto them that look for him* (wait for Him) *shall he appear the second time without sin unto salvation.*
>
> *Hebrews 9:28*

The Church Will Not Be Surprised

In the twenty-fourth chapter of Matthew our Lord spoke these words to His disciples:

> Watch, therefore: for ye know not what hour your Lord doth come.

> But know this, that if the goodman of the house had known in what watch the thief would come, he would have watched, and would not have suffered his house to be broken up.

> Therefore be ye also ready: for in such an hour as ye think not the Son of man cometh.
>
> *Matthew 24:42-44*

Even though it is very plain that Jesus is teaching here of judgment and punishment, it also behooves the Church in these last days to be watching her relationship with God and with each other so she will not fail to be ready for His return and thus suffer the dire results of unpreparedness.

This later warning of Jesus would perhaps be more fitting for the Christian Church as we draw near to the Rapture:

> Watch and pray, that ye enter not into temptation: the spirit indeed is willing, but the flesh is weak.
>
> *Matthew 26:41*

Remember also Paul's words:

Wherefore let him that thinketh he standeth take heed lest he fall.
1 Corinthians 10:12

The child of God must continually resist evil and never trust the flesh. **The days prior to the Rapture will be perilous times.** The Antichrist is ready to take over, and we must watch so we do not get caught up in material things, too much entertainment and not enough prayer, too much food and not enough fasting. Watch for your own soul, and stay close to Jesus and your brothers and sisters in Christ.

We, the Church, will continue to occupy, even as Jesus instructed. We will continue to witness, even more courageously. I have noticed that those who are preparing for the Antichrist by storing food, and even searching out caves in which to hide, have lost their zeal for seeing souls saved. They are thinking only of their own survival. Let us who look for the Rapture not become slack in our quest for souls, but be more zealous than ever before.

6
Confusion Surrounding Matthew 24

6
Confusion Surrounding Matthew 24

To the so-called prophecy specialists, Matthew 24 is a "sacred cow." It is not to be touched in order that their own viewpoints should not be disproved. According to them, it is a chapter that teaches great fear because of the things that are to come upon us prior to the Rapture. These "experts" say that these dire prophecies pertain to the Church — the Bride. I believe they greatly err.

Volumes have been written on this chapter. Hundreds of books have been published on this subject, and millions of dollars garnered from their sale. Almost all speakers and writers who teach that we, as a Church, will go through the Tribulation (the time of God's wrath — not persecution) draw the bulk of the material in support of their views from this chapter.

Matthew 24 begins with a question-and-answer time between the Lord and His disciples as they viewed Solomon's Temple and its many buildings. The disciples were very proud of their Jewish origin. They were also proud of the temple and what it stood for; and rightly so, for it represented the roots of the Jewish faith. You can imagine the excitement of the disciples as they talked with Jesus about the temple's sacred history and pointed out its glory and beauty. This conversation ends with the solemn announcement by the Lord Jesus that all they were looking at, including the city of Jerusalem, would be destroyed.

Tell us, the disciples said referring to the destruction, *when shall these things be? and what shall be the sign of thy coming, and of the end of the world?* (v. 3). In literal Greek, the "end of the world" about which they asked is the "completion of the age." They expected this great climactic event to embrace only the Jews.

Many scholars believe that these are but three questions in one. The questions asked of our Lord concerning the destruction and His return to execute vengeance upon the enemy had nothing whatsoever to do with the Rapture of the Church or of the total Gentile Church Age of Grace. Our Lord never talked directly about the Day of Grace, when the Gentiles would be brought in and the Jews broken off because of their unbelief, as referred to by Paul in Romans 9-11. This omission is understandable, considering the extreme hatred between Jew and Gentile.

Can you imagine Jesus saying in the presence of the Jews, "These same Gentiles from Rome, who will destroy your temple, ravish your women, crucify a thousand Jews each night for months and take the remainder into slavery — these very same Gentiles will one day receive Me, be gloriously saved, and become a major part of My Bride"? No, not even by the farthest stretch of the imagination! Had He told the Jews such a thing, not only would they have refused His words, He could have incited a riot. So when talking to the Jews, our Lord concentrated on what was going to happen within a very short time (even within forty years) to the generation standing there before Him.

Therefore, Matthew 24 must be approached with the Jewish disciples in mind. Jesus answered their questions with a close view of what would happen in the near future; then He went on with a telescopic view of end-time truth, skipping over the Church Age. This does not mean that our Lord excluded the Church or Church Age from His teaching on a godly life, turning the other cheek, the principles of the Lord's Prayer (see author's book, *Praying Beyond God's Ability*), the Beatitudes and parables, or Kingdom authority.

There must be a precarious balance between the superdispensationalist and the extreme Kingdom theologian. Because one's theology takes him predominantly into the camp of the dispensationalist (i.e. Some believe the day of miracles is over), the message to the total Church by our Lord — that we possess the power to bind, loose, move mountains of difficulty, etc. — cannot be ignored. There must be a balance between the two. But we must accept that Jesus was definitely limited in what He could say to the Jews about the Gentiles. It did not dawn on them that when Jesus gave them John 3:16, *Whosoever believeth on him should not perish,* the "whosoever" would include Gentiles, whom they called dogs.

While there could be double meaning in some verses of this chapter — verses that could relate to both the Jews and the Church Age — it seems to me that Jesus skipped completely over the Gentile Church Age of Grace in Matthew 24. He talked of the destruction of Jerusalem and referred to His Second Coming **in judgment** to judge those who had persecuted His people.

> *And then shall appear the sign of the Son of man in heaven: and then shall all the tribes of the earth mourn, and they shall see the Son of man coming in the clouds of heaven with power and great glory.*
>
> *Matthew 24:30*

There are many references in this chapter to the destruction of Jerusalem. Josephus, the Jewish historian, describes the fulfillment of these passages. The city of Jerusalem was surrounded in May, AD 66. The temple was burned August 10, AD 70 — the same day and month it had been burned years before by the king of Babylon.

Jesus warned, and I am sure His words were repeated many times, that the Jews living in Judea were to flee to the mountains. (v. 16.) Those on the rooftops (the rooftops of Jewish homes were flat, and the people retreated to them in the cool of the evening) were not to stop to get anything from their houses when they fled. (v. 17.) Those in the field were not to return to their houses for additional clothing. (v. 18.) Jesus spoke woe to those women with child and instructed all Jews to pray that the destruction would not happen in winter or on the Sabbath day (as did the Yom Kippur War of 1972). (vv. 19,20.)

These warnings all referred to the fall of Jerusalem, not to the Rapture of the Church, and so cannot be applied to today. Even the days being shortened for the sake of the elect (v. 22) was fulfilled: If Titus, the Roman emperor, had not relented, no Jew would have survived.

Jesus could have been looking forward toward the end of the Church Age, however, and referring to His coming for the Church when He said, *For as the lightning cometh out of the east, and shineth even unto the west; so shall also the coming of the Son of man be* (v. 27).

> *Immediately AFTER the tribulation of those days shall the sun be darkened, and the moon shall not give her light, and the stars shall fall from heaven, and the powers of the heavens shall be shaken:*

> And then shall appear the sign of the
> Son of man in heaven: and then shall all the
> tribes of the earth mourn, and they shall see
> the Son of man coming in the clouds of
> heaven with power and great glory.
>
> *Matthew 24:29,30*

In his book now out of print, Dr. T. J. McCrossan concludes from an examination of the Greek text that Matthew 24:27 — *For as the lightning cometh out of the east, and shineth even unto the west; so shall also the coming of the Son of man be* — occurs at a different point in time from Matthew 24:29,30 (quoted above). This Second Coming is established by putting the time **after** the Tribulation. (v. 29.)

The other time ("as the lightning flashes" — see Chapter 8 regarding the speed of light) is established by the word *that: But of that day and hour knoweth no man...* (v. 36). This demonstrative Greek pronoun *ekeinos* is always used to designate one of two persons or things mentioned previously, which is farthest removed from this pronoun. That is why the coming of the Lord for the Church in an atomic second is different from His coming **after** the Rapture. If His coming after the Tribulation had been inferred, then the pronoun *houtos* (this) would have been used.

Space will not permit a verse-by-verse explanation of Matthew 24. Jesus simply skipped over the Church Age by talking about the destruction

74

of Jerusalem, the false prophets (who did arise), the coldness and iniquity (which did occur), and giving warnings to the people not to take time to return to their homes but to flee. Then immediately He referred to events that were to happen prior to His Second Coming in judgment.

Notice in verses 29 and 30 that He skipped over the seven years of the Tribulation and discussed His coming in full power.

> *Now learn a parable of the fig tree; When his branch is yet tender, and putteth forth leaves, ye know that summer is nigh:*
>
> *So likewise ye, when ye shall see all these things, know that it is near, even at the doors.*
>
> *Verily I say unto you, THIS GENERA-TION shall not pass, til all these things be fulfilled.*
>
> Matthew 24:32-34

In these verses Jesus was referring to the restoration of the Jewish nation in 1948, saying that those who saw the restoration of that nation (*this generation*) would be living at the end.

Matthew 24:36 — *But of that day and hour knoweth no man, no, not the angels of heaven, but my Father only* — can be a reference to final judgment when Christ shall judge the kingdoms of this world. It is not necessarily a reference to the Rapture. (See 1 Thess. 5:4 for a reference to the Rapture and the fact that the Church **will not** be caught by surprise.) Verses 37 through 51 refer to the judgment.

Matthew 24 could have some dual applications. Some references could apply to the Christian Church, especially those verses regarding our being ready for His return and those that prophesy the Gospel being preached in all the world.

But, in my opinion, in this chapter Jesus was clearly speaking to the disciples about Jerusalem and its destruction, His Second Coming, and severe judgment. It is not a chapter from which to teach fear and to rob the Christians of their blessed hope.

7
The Book of Revelation

7
The Book of Revelation

And I turned to see the voice that spake
with me. And being turned, I saw seven
golden candlesticks;

And in the midst of the seven candlesticks one like unto the Son of man, clothed
with a garment down to the foot, and girt
about the paps with a golden girdle.

His head and his hairs were white like
wool, as white as snow; and his eyes were
as a flame of fire;

And his feet like unto fine brass, as if
they burned in a furnace; and his voice as
the sound of many waters.

And he had in his right hand seven
stars: and out of his mouth went a sharp
two-edged sword: and his countenance was
as the sun shineth in his strength.

Revelation 1:12-16

This description of Jesus, as John saw Him in the
Spirit, is one good reason why one cannot prove any
doctrine on the last days **by this book alone.** What

John saw in the Spirit and tried to relate in human terms can only be understood symbolically.

The book of Revelation was not meant to be taken literally. Jesus, our Lord and Savior, does not have eyes that are flames of fire. Certainly He does not have a two-edged sword shooting out His mouth, and I trust that those seven stars He holds in His right hand are symbolic, not literal.

Nevertheless, certain truths expressed in symbolic language can also have definite literal meanings. John did see Jesus Christ; all the things he described about Him in symbolic language do have meanings that are literally true. Jesus is the Son of God, He is a judge, He speaks the Word as a two-edged sword, and He holds in His hands the power of heaven. Already scripturally established doctrine can be confirmed by symbolic language; however, we cannot find the foundation for pet doctrines in the book of Revelation.

The seven churches addressed by John were literal churches in John's day, and were probably under his care. To make these churches represent seven Church periods, as the dispensationalist does, however, will not be successful. Most dispensationalists use the Laodicean church, because it is the last mentioned (Rev. 3:14-22), to describe the Church that will be on the earth when Jesus returns for His Bride.

This was my understanding from the many books I had read on the subject, and, as a result, I believed it for many years. Therefore, I fully expected the church I pastored to become lukewarm and backslidden, along with the other churches. This was further reinforced by the teaching I received on the "falling away":

> *Let no man deceive you by any means: for that day (the Rapture) shall not come, except there come a falling away first, and that man of sin be revealed, the son of perdition.*
>
> *2 Thessalonians 2:3*

I have since come to understand that the Greek word *apostasia* can be translated "departure" instead of "falling away" (and has been by many scholars). This discovery sent me back to the book of Revelation to reexamine the seven letters to the seven churches.

Will the Church that is to be raptured be a Laodicean church, or could it be one of the other six? Symbolically, the latter could be true. The Lord instructed the church at Sardis to watch, or else He, Jesus, would come upon them as a thief (this, of course, in judgment). (Rev. 3:1-6.)

Any time the Lord likened His coming to that of a thief, it was usually a warning of judgment, not deliverance. (See Rev. 3:3; Matt. 24:43; 1 Thess. 5:2; and 2 Pet. 3:10.)

Paul told the Thessalonians that they, the Church, would not be overtaken as by a thief. (1 Thess. 5:4.) They would, therefore, have to recognize something that would precede His coming, otherwise they would be surprised. There is only one church of the seven for which Jesus promised to come. This church had not denied His name and was told to hold fast so the enemy would not rob them. This one church was the church in Philadelphia (Rev. 3:7-13), and I believe this one represents the day in which we are now living.

This last-day church experiences great revival. There is such a movement of God that even the enemies from the synagogue (meeting place) of Satan come and bow in defeat to the last-day church. (v. 9.) Why? So all will know how much God loves these last-day believers. And, along with my brothers, I am beginning to experience this revival, and I fully expect it to grow.

Notice, too, that this church is also keeping the word of His patience. (v. 10.) That is, they are looking for His coming. This sounds like many of us today who are expecting Him. *Be patient therefore, brethren, unto the coming of the Lord* (James 5:7).

The Lord also promised that they (the Church which is looking for His coming) will be kept from the hour or time (*hora*) of temptation or trial (*peirasmos*) which is to come upon all the **world**: *Because you have patiently obeyed me despite the persecution,*

82

therefore I will protect you from the time of great
tribulation and temptation, which will come upon the
world to test everyone alive. (Rev. 3:10,
paraphrased.)

The Greek reads, *ek tes horas,* meaning "out of,
or clean away from, the hour or time set" for that
Tribulation. Revelation 3:10 also confirms 2 Peter
2:9: *The Lord knoweth how to deliver the godly out of
temptations, and to reserve the unjust unto the day of
judgment to be punished.* (The same Greek word
peirasmos, meaning temptation or trial or
tribulation, is used here.) Peter tells how the Lord
will do this: by *rhuesthoi,* the present infinitive of the
deponent Greek verb *rhuomai,* meaning "to deliver
by drawing a person to one's self out of harm's way"
(McCrossan). From what is God going to deliver His
people? From the great day of His wrath!

> For the great day of his wrath is come;
> and who shall be able to stand?
>
> *Revelation 6:17*

The Greek word for wrath is *orge,* which means
"justifiable violent passion; ire; anger." Read the
following to confirm that we will not be here to
experience the wrath of God:

> *Much more then, having been now
> justified by his blood* (literal), *we shall be
> saved from wrath* (orge) *through him*
> (Christ).
>
> *Romans 5:9*

> *And to wait for his Son from heaven, whom he raised from the dead, even Jesus, which delivered* (literally, "the one delivering") *us from the wrath to come* (apo tes or ges tes erchomenes, "from the wrath" or "the coming wrath").
>
> 1 Thessalonians 1:10

> *For God hath not appointed us to wrath, but to obtain salvation* (soteria, "deliverance") *by our Lord Jesus Christ.*
>
> 1 Thessalonians 5:9

I believe the church at Philadelphia represents the last-day Church, to whom the Lord said, *I come quickly* (Rev. 3:11). The Laodicean church, the unsaved church, is the lukewarm church that makes God sick to His stomach, and He spews them out. (v. 16.) Jesus stands outside the door, knocking (v. 20), but they will not let Him in. This is the church, along with other unsaved churches, that will have to enter into the Jewish seventieth week, not the redeemed and believing Church. The redeemed Church, the Bride of Christ, is spared God's wrath and is taken up in the Rapture before the time of the Great Tribulation.

Revelation 4 pictures the Church in heaven, placing the Rapture after chapter 3 and making it precede all events to follow on earth, including the opening of the seals and the ensuing judgments.

One of the proofs, to me, that the Church **will not be on earth during the Tribulation** is that John sees the twenty-four elders in heaven (Rev. 4:4), and they are still there in Revelation 19:4. Up to this point, elders have always been on the earth; now they are in heaven in their new bodies. The Greek word *presbuteros* (masculine gender), translated "elders," by its very definition indicates those who are "elderly, aged, senior." If that is the case, then these beings are subject to age. As such then, they are definitely **not** spirit beings because spirit beings are ageless. Those who ascribe to the post-Tribulation position believe that these are spirit creatures. This interpretation is necessary to support their belief that the Church will be on earth during the Tribulation described after Revelation 3.

Notice in Revelation 11:16 that these elders fall on their faces and worship God. The Greek word for faces here is *prosopon*, meaning "**human** faces." In Revelation 5:9, the saints sing that Jesus *hast redeemed us to God*. The verse (well supported by the Greek text) reads "hast redeemed **us**." Some who hold the post-Tribulation position make it to read, "hast redeemed **them**," as though the saints were yet to be redeemed and not already in heaven.

Notice, too, in Revelation 19:5 that these elders are also called "servants" (*doulos*). Spirit beings are never called servants. Only the believers (the

Church) are called servants. (Eph. 6:5; Phil. 1:1;
1 Pet. 2:16.)

The four beasts mentioned with the elders
appear to be symbolic of the Gospel message. (Rev.
4:7.) They do not seem to have the same identity as
the elders. They seem to assist God in whatever He is
doing. In the Old Testament Ezekiel saw these same
creatures in heaven, but not the elders because they
were not yet there. (Ezek. 1:4-25.)

I also believe that in chapter 4 the Church, the
Bride, has **already** been to the Judgment Seat of
Christ, and has **already been rewarded**. They have
the crowns on their heads (*stephanos*, "victor's
wreaths," which are meant for human, not spirit,
beings) and are wearing fine linen, white and clean.
In 2 Timothy 4:8, Paul said, *There is laid up for me a
crown* (a *stephanos*). In 1 Thessalonians 2:19 the
redeemed saints are promised crowns.

The Judgment Seat of Christ will probably take
place in heaven during the first half of Daniel's
seventieth week (the three and one-half years during
which the Antichrist rules in peace and full power,
deceiving the whole earth). Remember, this week of
seven years is for the Jews, not for the Church.

What about the Tribulation saints mentioned in
Revelation 20:4? In his commentary Adam Clark
states: "These are they who represent all that have
been martyred through the ages." They do not have

crowns of gold. They were not overcomers, as were the true saints, and the only reward for their martyrdom is to reign with Christ for a thousand years. (See Chapter 3 entitled *Rapture and Resurrection.*) They are not identified with the Bride in any way.

I personally believe that the Tribulation martyrs (Rev. 20:4; 6:9-11) are not born again because they do not seem to carry the same spirit as the Church. They cry out for God to avenge them speedily. (v. 10.) They want to see their enemies dealt with harshly. The cry of the martyred born-again saint (for example, Stephen in Acts 7:60) was the same as that of the Lord Jesus: *Father, forgive them; for they know not what they do* (Luke 23:34).

What a vast gulf divides the Tribulation saints from the Bride! They don't seem to have a spirit of love and forgiveness as do the martyrs in the New Testament. These martyred saints seem to attain heaven by dying for God. I believe they are mostly Jewish people who will tenaciously hold to their belief in an eternal God, no matter what the cost or whether they believe as Christians do. There will no doubt be some Gentiles among them because of the witness they give. This, however, should not give a false hope to a backslider.

The seventh angel, sounding a trumpet in Revelation 11:15, is used by both the mid-Tribulation and post-Tribulation proponents to support their belief that the Rapture takes place at this point rather than at the beginning of Revelation 4. However, a casual reading will reveal that this judgment of the nations is prior to the Millenium, or even after all is over, because verse 18 speaks of the final judgment and destruction recorded by Peter in 2 Peter 3:10-13.

Remember, when Christ returns to sit in judgment at the seventh trump, we are already rewarded and come **with Him**, as Jude records in verse 14: *Behold, the Lord cometh with ten thousands of his saints.*

Literally volumes could be written as to what the true interpretation of the book of Revelation is. All sides in the argument will try to prove their points and make the book say whatever fits their predetermined arguments. Sometimes even the more clearly marked scriptures end up being clouded and confused in the presentation.

The Church, as the Bride, and her Rapture can best be understood by staying with what the Apostle Paul wrote from his personal revelations as given to him by our Lord Jesus. He alone was shown the Rapture. He wrote about it, thus settling all various and sundry opinions once and for all. **The Church is not appointed for wrath, but to obtain deliverance by our Lord Jesus Christ.** (1 Thess. 5:9.) These were Paul's words of hope to the believers of his day, and thus to all of us who wait for His appearing. What a hope! So keep on hoping!

8
As The Lightning . . .

8
As The Lightning . . .

I tell you this, my brothers: an earthly body made of flesh and blood cannot get into God's kingdom. These perishable bodies of ours are not the right kind to live forever.

But I am telling you this strange and wonderful secret: we shall not all die, but we shall all be given new bodies!

It will all happen in a moment, in the twinkling of an eye, when the last trumpet is blown. For there will be a trumpet blast from the sky and all the Christians who have died will suddenly become alive, with new bodies that will never, never die; and then we who are still alive shall suddenly have new bodies too.

For our earthly bodies, the ones we have now that can die, must be transformed into heavenly bodies that cannot perish but will live forever.

When this happens, then at last this Scripture will come true—"Death is swallowed up in victory."

> *O death, where then your victory?
> Where then your sting? For sin—the sting
> that causes death—will all be gone; and the
> law, which reveals our sins, will no longer
> be our judge.*
>
> *How we thank God for all of this! It is
> he who makes us victorious through Jesus
> Christ our Lord!*
>
> *1 Corinthians 15:50-57* LB

Paul's revelation and authority received from the Lord Jesus concerning the Rapture was shared with the Corinthian church as well as with the Thessalonians. It is a thrilling comparison to read the above and then to recall the Lord's discourse in Matthew 24 where He compared His coming to lightning. It is reasonable that Jesus should compare His coming to light, which comes from heaven and is as fast as lightning, inasmuch as in the beginning of our Bible God said, *Let there be light* (Gen. 1:3), and 1 John 1:5 says, *God is light.*

Scientists now know much more about light, its speed and its relationship to time, because of Einstein's discovery of the Law of Relativity: $E = MC^2$. Not only was it a major breakthrough for the invention and production of the first atomic bomb, but it also revealed secrets of creation.

With this increased knowledge, a new understanding opened up concerning earth's time relative to the speed of light. Simply stated, time becomes a decreasing factor as one begins to approach the speed of light.

As we have seen, the Bible pictures God as being Light. (1 John 1:5.) The amazing speed of light — 186,272 miles per second — is equal to 6 million million (5.88 trillion) miles in one year. We find this difficult to visualize unless we bring it down to our measure of comprehension.

Let me illustrate: If you were to wind up an old-fashioned alarm clock and count the tick-tocks for 32 thousand years, you would count a total of 1 million million. Yet light travels **6** million million miles in one year. In one hour it travels 670 million miles. If you were to fire a rifle whose bullet would travel the speed of light, it would travel around the circumference of the earth over seven times before you could remove your finger from the trigger.

Accepting the fact, then, that light comes from God, we can say that if one were to travel at an accelerating speed approaching the speed of light, he would be moving from the time dimension toward the eternal dimension. As one continues to accelerate, time slows. If you could travel at the speed of light, time would stop. This is called the "time dialation" theory and is based on Einstein's Law of Relativity.

If you were to travel in a spaceship at 87 percent the speed of light, time would slow by 50 percent. This could be illustrated with the help of a little imagination. Think of yourself in a spaceship traveling at 87 percent the speed of light. You could travel into outer space for twenty years, turn your spaceship around and return to earth, having been gone a total of forty years. Imagine your surprise when you stepped out of your spaceship and discovered that everyone on earth had aged — and those who had been your age when you left are now twice as old as you are!

If you were to step this up until you were traveling at 99.99 percent the speed of light and traveled into outer space for a total of sixty years, when you returned you would find that five million years had passed while you were gone.

Yes, if you could travel at 100 percent the speed of light, **time would stop and the moment "now" would be forever** — for that is where God's throne is and where the timeless, eternal dimension exists.

If you are wondering what is faster than light, you may recall that the Lord's return to take us out of this world is going to be in an atomic second. As we read previously:

> *Behold, I shew you a mystery; We shall not all sleep, but we shall all be changed,*
>
> *In a MOMENT (atomos), in the twinkling of an eye, at the last trump . . . .*
> *1 Corinthians 15:51,52*

The *King James Version* translates the Greek word *atomos* ("atomic") as "moment" or "twinkling of an eye." The Lord will take us out of this world so fast that time will stop and the moment "now" will be forever for us. There will be no aging in heaven, no more of time's depredations. When the trumpet shall sound, time will be no more for the saint of God. The dead shall go first, and then the living shall be changed. What a glorious event that will be!

Paul told the Corinthians the same things he taught the Thessalonians: the dead go first, then the living. I believe, with you, that "we who are still alive" refers to us living today. You might say, "All Christians have believed this since the fathers fell asleep," which is true, but then technology had not yet developed the hydrogen bomb and Israel was not in her homeland, Palestine. The scene was not set for the take-over of the Antichrist, nor was there an alinement of ten nations in the European Common Market as there is today.

We must be drawing very close to that last trump, which will signal the first coming of our Lord for His Church. This trumpet sound differs from the last trump in Revelation. As Greek scholars explain, if it were the last trumpet to sound, there would have to be a definite article preceding the word *trumpet*. Also, the last trumpet in Revelation is a signal for other events to follow. In 1 Corinthians 15:52, the trumpet blast and the Rapture are simultaneous events. This is brought out by the Greek preposition *en*, meaning "right then."

In an atomic second we will rise to meet our wonderful Lord. I believe it is worthy of note that in the history of the Church, there has been great poverty and suffering, and it was only natural for the believers to want their Lord to rescue them from their suffering. Even today, many saints who suffer behind prison walls anticipate the Rapture as a blessed release.

However, in the last of this twentieth century, the majority of the saints live in great ease in a land of plenty. Yet, in the midst of the luxury, the Christians I know are watching for the Lord's return, not to escape persecution or suffering, but just because they love Him and so desire to be with Him. This modern, twentieth-century style of easy living does not satisfy our hearts. The longing and hunger to be with Him, our Lord, is in our spirits and cannot be filled by things that are only temporal. The Rapture is not meant to be an "escape hatch" but a gigantic step from the physical into that glorious spiritual realm.

All distance is measured by time. If you are going toward a destination, as you run out of time allotted, you run out of distance. God's plan of the ages is running out of time, thus we are runniung out of distance. Every day brings us closer to our Lord's coming and eternity in His presence.

9
America In Prophecy

9
America In Prophecy

It has never seemed probable to many Christians that a nation as great as America would be without mention in the Scriptures. It never seemed right to me that God would not mention a nation that has done so much for missions and also for His people, Israel.

Even as a young minister I believed that America must be mentioned somewhere in prophecy; and because of this belief, I made a diligent study of all biblical references that could possibly allude to our great land. If America is mentioned, it would, of course, have to be in symbolic language; and if it is in prophecy, then, in my opinion, it would have to be in Isaiah 18.

Woe to the land shadowing with wings, which is beyond the rivers of Ethiopia:

That sendeth ambassadors by the sea, even in vessels of bulrushes upon the waters, saying, Go, ye swift messengers, to a nation scattered and peeled, to a people terrible from their beginning hitherto; a nation meted out and trodden down, whose land the rivers have spoiled!

Another Look At The Rapture

All ye inhabitants of the world, and dwellers on the earth, see ye, when he lifteth up an ensign on the mountains; and when he bloweth a trumpet, hear ye.

For so the Lord said unto me, I will take my rest, and I will consider in my dwelling place like a clear heat upon herbs, and like a cloud of dew in the heat of harvest.

For afore the harvest, when the bud is perfect, and the sour grape is ripening in the flower, he shall both cut off the sprigs with pruning hooks, and take away and cut down the branches.

They shall be left together unto the fowls of the mountains, and to the beasts of the earth: and the fowls shall summer upon them, and all the beasts of the earth shall winter upon them.

In that time shall the present be brought unto the Lord of hosts of a people scattered and peeled, and from a people terrible from their beginning hitherto; a nation meted out and trodden under foot, whose land the rivers have spoiled, to the place of the name of the Lord of hosts, the mount Zion.

Isaiah 18:1-7

Why do I believe that this particular chapter relates to America? First, because Adam Clark and Matthew Henry both agree in their commentaries that the country mentioned in verse 1 as being *beyond the rivers of Ethiopia* is difficult, if not impossible, to trace; i.e. they don't believe it was a country known in that day, which helps us to receive that it could be a country of our day. Adam Clark states:

"This is one of the most obscure prophecies in the whole book of Isaiah. The subject of it, the end and the design of it, the people to whom it is addressed, the history to which it belongs, the person who sends the messengers, and the nation to whom the messengers are sent are all obscure and doubtful." Its description does not fit any country or region of that day.

One cannot be literal in all methods of interpretation. There must be some symbolic meanings inferred. Most books on prophecy written through the years that set forth as literal all passages of Scripture have long since been discredited. So let us explore this chapter from the vantage point or symbolism and see what conclusions can be reached.

First, notice that this land must send ambassadors by sea because of its location. (v. 2.) That is, it does not have access to Israel by land. This would rule out most of the nations that were known in Isaiah's day. Thus, the land is far away. Also this land is *shadowed with wings* (v. 1), which calls to mind the fact that America has always been symbolized by eagles.

Second, notice that it is a land divided, or "spoiled," by rivers. (v. 2.) *Spoiled* can also mean "nourished." America, a land of rivers, is the only large landmass that is crisscrossed by many rivers. Most nations are known for their one outstanding river: in Brazil, the Amazon; in China, the Yantze; in Egypt, the Nile.

Third, notice the people. There are a nation of leaders. The nation was *terrible* (awesome) *from its beginning* and was always successful in war. (v. 2.) America, overnight, was a leading nation of the world. She defeated England and took her destiny into her own hands. She became a nation which demanded attention when she spoke (v. 3), a nation to be reckoned with.

Fourth, the inhabitants are tall, bronzed, and "peeled" or clean shaven. (v. 2.) It is said that America was the first nation to make the razor part of the standard equipment in the militaryman's kit. *A nation meted out and trodden down* (v. 2) suggests a land of great population. America has one of the largest populations in the world today.

Finally, verses 4 and 5 speak of the great harvest and productivity of this great nation in the very height of its achievement and how at the peak of its productivity (*when the bud is perfect*) it is cut down. America has now reached its zenith, and in some respects, is showing the first little indications of a decline in leadership as an industrial nation. The nation mentioned in Isaiah 18 as being at the height of productivity is so utterly destroyed that there are not enough people left to bury the dead. *They shall be left together unto the fowls of the mountains, and to the beasts of the earth* (v. 6). Could this refer to the aftermath of a neutron bomb?

The news media has made it clear that Russia possesses enough hydrogen bombs, and the hardware to deliver them, to devastate America. Russia knows that America, if given a few more years with her present rebuilding program, will equal her in the arms race. When will she attack us? Of course, this must be in the knowledge and timing of the Lord, but her threats to bury us cannot be ignored. Neither can the fact that when Russia comes down from the north, there is no one to help Israel; America must be out of the picture as the Lord is the One Who steps in to help her.

The last verse of Isaiah 18 is the one which convinces me that this chapter not only refers to America, but also makes reference to the Church. Verse 7 mentions a present, a gift that will be given to the Lord of Hosts from this nation that is so utterly destroyed there are not enough survivors to bury the dead. This has never happened. A completely destroyed nation is in no condition or position to bring a gift to the Lord.

But it will happen when the Rapture occurs. What a gift to the Lord of Hosts to receive so many of His people coming home! What a blessed event it will be! The trumpet will sound, the gift (the redeemed Church) will rise to meet the Lord, and so shall she ever be with Him!

What will then happen to America? Use your imagination. If God allows our present-day revival to continue and all our loved ones are saved, there will be so many people going home that there won't be many left. The ones who are left might not be in strategic positions to defend or lead America; she will be vulnerable to a devastating missile attack.

Why do I believe this? Because Russia has threatened to bury us. She is desperate for oil and industrial world leadership. She cannot risk being counterattacked by a strong nation. But when she hears of the confusion caused by the Rapture, she will strike quickly.

When the Antichrist takes over, he will have no opposition. Israel will be defenseless; she will have no friends. America will be gone.

Yes, reader, believe on and receive the Lord Jesus Christ as your Savior! Get ready for a great home-going. You do not want to be here after the

Church and the Holy Spirit are removed and America is destroyed. Believe now and receive Him. You have a choice: You can go with the Church, or be left to the fowls of the mountains as your only burial.

10
Believing For Our Loved Ones

10
Believing For Our Loved Ones

This book on the Rapture would never have been written if its purpose was to get people excited or to propose the Rapture as an "out" for people who want to avoid paying their bills, getting up and going to work, or facing another day of housecleaning or school. My motive, above all else, is to stir you, to rouse you to believe and pray as never before for the salvation of your loved ones.

No promise from God is ever automatic. You will be God's partner in every spiritual transaction, or there will be none. John Wesley has been quoted as saying: "God does nothing but by prayer."

If, as some theologians teach us, salvation is by election and not for "whosoever will," then all of us have wasted our time in thinking we have a chance to make heaven our home. If God pre-selects those He wants to be with Him forever and those who are destined for hell, then why would He send Jesus? His suffering would be of no value.

God is big enough to do as He wants without us. He could have given a blanket pardon for the ones to whom He is partial and, in one fell swoop, could have swept all others into hell. But, no, it is yet *whosoever believeth in him should not perish, but have everlasting life* (John 3:16), and it always will be. There must be the believing and the receiving of God's plan of redemption. There has to be, in the human heart, a love for God, a love for His people, a love for the things He loves, and a hatred for the things He hates.

God is sovereign in His kingdom and in the choosing of nations. He, looking ahead, chose a nation when He chose Jacob over Esau. (Gen. 25:23.) He saw, by foreknowledge, that Esau would despise his birthright; and even though Jacob was a conniver, God saw a spiritual hunger in him. He saw Jacob wrestling with the angel and refusing to let go until he had received a blessing. (Gen. 32:24-26.)

The key verses which teach us that we have something to do with God's decisions are found in Romans 11 and Acts 16:

> *Well; because of unbelief they (the Jews) were broken off, and thou standest by faith. Be not highminded, but fear:*

> *For if God spared not the natural branches, take heed lest he also spare not thee.*

> *Behold therefore the goodness and severity of God: on them which fell, severity;*

but toward thee, goodness, if thou continue in his goodness: otherwise thou also shalt be cut off.

And they also, if they abide not still in unbelief, shall be grafted in: for God is able to graft them in again.

Romans 11:20-23

And they (Paul and Silas) said (to the Philippian jailer), Believe on the Lord Jesus Christ, and thou shalt be saved, and thy house.

And they spake unto him the word of the Lord, and to all that were in his house.

And he took them the same hour of the night, and washed their stripes; and was baptized, he and all his, straightway.

And when he had brought them into his house, he sat meat before them, and rejoiced, believing in God with all his house.

Acts 16:31-34

These significant verses teach us that if the head of the house believes on the Lord Jesus, there is a promise that all the house will be saved. In the case of the Philippian jailer, this was so.

"But," you may say, "I'm not the head of my house. My husband is." Then your promise is found in 1 Corinthians 7:13-16:

111

And the woman which hath an husband that believeth not, and if he be pleased to dwell with her, let her not leave him.

For the unbelieving husband is sanctified by the wife, and the unbelieving wife is sanctified by the husband: else were your children unclean; but now are they holy.

But if the unbelieving depart, let him depart. A brother or a sister is not under bondage in such cases: but God hath called us to peace.

For what knowest thou, O wife, whether thou shalt save thy husband? or how knowest thou, O man, whether thou shalt save thy wife?

These scriptures confirm God's great compassion for the family. He does not want to see one member saved and another lost. Make no mistake, God is a family-loving Father.

Let us deal with 1 Corinthians 7:13-16 first, and then go back to Acts 16:31-34. The promise that the unsaved husband or wife is sanctified by living with the Christian counterpart is a precise and straight-forward declaration of what will happen. Not maybe, probably, possibly — but *will happen*. The only condition here is that the saved wife or husband lead a godly life. (See also 1 Pet. 3:1-7.) Yes, in two places God has promised that the husband and wife, if they stay married and are pleased with their marriage, shall both be saved. Great emphasis should be placed on the word *pleased*. Both husband and wife must watch their conversation. They must talk like a child of God. There should be no nagging, scolding, or faultfinding — and there certainly should not be preaching in the home.

You, a husband or wife living with a mate who is not presently saved, should get on your knees and thank God for His Word and for the assurance that you will see your mate in heaven. Now go your way rejoicing and acting as though your mate is now a Christian. Talk like it, act like it, and be happy about it. Give thanks for it now as you will on the day it happens.

God considers the unsaved spouses to be already saved when He declares the children of such marriages to be sanctified, *else were your children unclean; but now are they holy* (1 Cor. 7:14). Only by one member of the marriage deserting the other would the promise be broken. If one partner leaves, God declares the marriage to be broken, and the born-again spouse is free from the bondage of that union. (There are absolutely no grounds scripturally for a Christian spouse to ever seek a divorce except for desertion or infidelity.) (Matt. 19:9.)

Concerning the children of a broken home, the ones staying with the Christian parent will benefit from God's promise. The ones choosing to go with the unsaved parent and live that lifestyle will reap the uncleanness accompanying their decision. However, if the children were forced to go with the unregenerate parent, the saved spouse can claim salvation for them.

You might ask (because you are not the head of your house), "What about my unsaved parents?" If you are the first member, or the only member, of your house to be saved, then you can act in authority as the priest of that house until others are saved.

The following, based on Acts 16:30,31, is how to pray for the unsaved members of your family. Your family (or house) includes only those under your direct influence, such as husband, wife, daughter, son, sister, brother, parents, or grandparents. In the Old Testament, when the destroyer smote the first-born, all that were in the house where the blood of the lamb had been applied to the doorposts were saved. You, too, must enter into a covenant promise, a contract, by becoming part of its stipulations. You must, at a specific time and place, declare yourself to enter into this agreement. No promise is automatic. Your name must be present in the agreement.

Call on a believer to agree with you in prayer when you enter into this specific contract with God concerning your loved ones.

Your prayer could be something like this:

My dear Heavenly Father, in Jesus' name, I come to You on behalf of my loved ones. I thank You that You have promised me in Acts 16:31 of Your Word (open your Bible and read it aloud) that if I would believe on You, not only will I be saved, but all the members of my house. I thank You that I know You keep Your Word, and I now enter into this covenant.

I am trusting You, dear Holy Spirit, to do Your work, and I believe I will see them in heaven. Amen.

When the Rapture takes place, there will not be the normal time of natural death with time for repentance. Our loved ones must get saved **now**. When the trumpet sounds, it will be too late.

If you have raised your children in the way of the Lord, but they seem to be wandering from His path at this time, let this scripture be a comfort to you:

Thus saith the Lord; Refrain thy voice from weeping, and thine eyes from tears: for thy work shall be rewarded, saith the Lord; and they shall come again from the land of the enemy.

And there is hope in thine end, saith the Lord, that thy children shall come again to their own border.

Jeremiah 31:16,17

Summary

Paul's letters to the church in Thessalonica were more than a lifeline of hope. They imparted great revelation concerning God's attitude toward the Church and toward the human family, as a family unit. They also reveal His attitude toward a man coming into power who will be completely possessed by Satan. The one called the "man of sin." (2 Thess. 2:3.)

God's revealed attitude toward His Church, His people, is one of unsurpassed love. Not only does He love us, He greatly desires for us to be with Him forever.

Some people, arguing against the hope of the Rapture, believe that because the Church has not always taught and emphasized this truth, it is only a "Johnny-come-lately" doctrine. It has even been hinted that this is an American theological dream.

The doctrine of the Resurrection of the dead and the Rapture of the living has always been believed and written about. It was not emphasized for many centuries, and rightly so, because the Church then was hundreds of years away from the time it would happen. Also, then, as now, there was confusion between the Rapture and the Second

Coming of our Lord. In the Rapture we rise to meet Him; in the Second Coming He comes to the earth to rule and to reign.

In regard to this great truth of the Rapture not being emphasized in certain periods of Church history, we must acknowledge that other great truths were also submerged at times. Justification by faith, baptism of the Holy Spirit, glossalalia, and divine healing in the Atonement were hidden from view during some periods of history. It is only right and proper for the Holy Spirit to greatly emphasize this great truth now because of the imminence of events leading up to a catastrophic climax.

In this summary, let me emphasize chapter 4 which deals with the Greek word *apostasia*. To say that it can only be translated one way (i.e., "falling away" or "rebellion"), greatly conflicts with God's Word which says that in the last days He will pour out His Spirit on all flesh. (Acts 2:17.) To translate this word as "departure" coincides better with the rest of Paul's message which gave great hope to his readers when all hope was gone.

For Paul to write that the Church, prior to the coming of the Lord Jesus in the skies, would completely rebel and backslide, would have further **added** to the Thessalonians' **sorrow** and **confusion**, and would have taken away what **little hope** they had.

Summary

While I stated that we cannot build a doctrine on how one Greek word is translated, it certainly must be recognized by the post-Tribulation writers as having some meaning pertinent to the interpretation of Paul's revelation received from our Lord Jesus and to other promises concerning great revival in the last days.

The interpretation of Scripture can be compared to **skating on thin ice**. At best, one is always in danger of breaking through into a cold bath, or even death. If one is too much of a literalist, he becomes too heavy and will surely break through. If he is too symbolic, he is too light and will be blown off his course. If he is a firm dispensationalist and can only skate in one direction, he is bound to fall into some of the very same theological holes that others have fallen into.

If he is an antidispensationalist, he does not know where he has been; therefore, he cannot know where he is going. If he leans too heavily on higher education, he will be above the greater percentage of the people to whom he will be ministering. If he is against academic achievement, he may not be open to more illumination and, therefore, in danger of becoming unteachable.

All of us must be open and receptive, and strive for more balance. If a weakness can be pointed out in that which we have so strongly believed, let us be humble enough to admit that further light has come and that we are open to change.

I trust that I will always remain open to further enlightenment. After diligent study and research on this great subject, I firmly believe that **before** the worst is to come, what Paul so wonderfully described by the impulse of the Holy Spirit will take place:

The Lord himself shall descend from heaven with a shout, with the voice of the archangel, and with the trump of God: and the dead in Christ shall rise first:

Then we which are alive and remain shall be caught up together with them in the clouds, to meet the Lord in the air: and so shall we ever be with the Lord.

1 Thessalonians 4:16,17

References

The Amplified Bible. Published by Zondervan Publishing House, Grand Rapids, Michigan. Used by permission.

An Expository Dictionary of New Testament Words. W. E. Vine. Published by Fleming H. Revell Company, Old Tappan, New Jersey. Used by permission.

Interlinear Greek-English New Testament. George Ricker Berry. Published by Baker Book House, Grand Rapids, Michigan. Used by permission.

The Living Bible. Published by Tyndale House Publishers, Wheaton, Illinois. Used by permission.

The New Testament — An Expanded Translation. Kenneth S. Wuest. Published by William B. Eerdmans Publishing Company, Grand Rapids, Michigan. Used by permission.

Roy H. Hicks is a successful minister of the Gospel who has given his life to pastoring and pioneering churches throughout the United States. He has served the Lord in various foreign fields, having made missionary journeys to South America, the Orient, Australia, and New Zealand.

As a dedicated man of God, Dr. Hicks serves today as General Supervisor of the Foursquare Gospel Churches and has become a popular speaker at charismatic conferences.

Perhaps the thing that most endears Dr. Hicks to readers is his warmth and his ability to reach out as the true believer he is — a man of strong, positive faith, sharing a refreshing ministry through the power and anointing of the Holy Spirit.

USE IT OR LOSE IT

by Dr. Roy Hicks

FAITH IS A GIFT FROM GOD

Unapplied faith gives way to unbelief.

May this book inspire us to exercise our faith and learn more perfectly how faith works. I have endeavoured to reveal its utter simplicity. I would like this presentation to be a source of great strength and help to all who read it.

Dr. Roy Hicks

Call now toll free and order this life-changing book!

1 800 331 3334